Lalin at the Market

by Arlène Elizabeth Casimir • illustrated by Shearry Malone

Lucy Calkins and Michael Rae-Grant, Series Editors

LETTER-SOUND CORRESPONDENCES

m, t, a, n, s, ss, p, i,
d, g, o, c, k, ck, r, u,
h, b, e, f, ff, l, ll, z,
j, v, w, y, qu

HIGH-FREQUENCY WORDS

is, like, see, the, no, so, too,
of, says, go, to, for, look,
me, be, you, she

Lalin at the Market
Author: Arlène Elizabeth Casimir
Series Editors: Lucy Calkins and Michael Rae-Grant

Heinemann
145 Maplewood Avenue, Suite 300
Portsmouth, NH 03801
www.heinemann.com

Cataloging-in-Publication data is on file with the Library of Congress.

ISBN-13: 978-0-325-13828-2

Design and Production: Dinardo Design LLC, Carole Berg, and Rebecca Anderson

Editors: Anna Cockerille and Jennifer McKenna

Illustrations: Shearry Malone

Photographs: p. 32 © Hemis/Alamy; inside back cover (kids) © Sergey Novikov/ Shutterstock; inside back cover (duck) © Dobbography/Shutterstock.

Manufacturing: Gerard Clancy

Printed in Dongguan, China
4 5 6 7 8 9 10 TP 28 27 26 25 24 23
April 2023 Printing / PO# 4500868396

Contents

Meet...

Lalin   Liv   Mom

Let's Go to the Market

Lalin, Liv, and Mom
go to the market.

"Can I get off?" asks Lalin.

Lalin tugs on Liv's hand.

"Quick, let's go!" she says.

Lalin sees big bags
and stops to look.

DJON DJON

Liv says, "Let's go, Lalin!"

Liv tugs and tugs on Lalin.

"Quit it!" says Mom.

"Yum, yum!

Can I, Mom?" Lalin asks.

"Me too?" Liv asks.

Lalin gets a zip lock bag.

Liv gets a bag too.

"Yum!" says Lalin.

"Not yum ... yuck!" says Liv.

"Hand it to me!

I like it!" says Lalin.

"Lalin," says Mom.

"You got a snack!

So hand it to me. I will like it!"

2

Lalin Gets Lost

"The market is fun!" says Lalin.

"No, it is not!" huffs Liv.

"It is SO dull."

"Quit it!" says Mom.

Lalin sees a bit of red silk.

"Look! It is a quilt!" gasps Lalin.

Lalin likes the soft, red quilt.

"Liv, look at it!" she says.

Lalin can not see Liv.

Lalin can not see Mom.

Lalin is lost!

So, she asks for help.

At last, Lalin spots

Mom and Liv.

She runs and gets a hug!

3

At the Market

You can go to the market.

It is fun!

It can be hot at the market.

It can be wet at the market.

You can get jam on a bun
and a cup to sip.

You can fill up a bag.

You will see pets and hens.

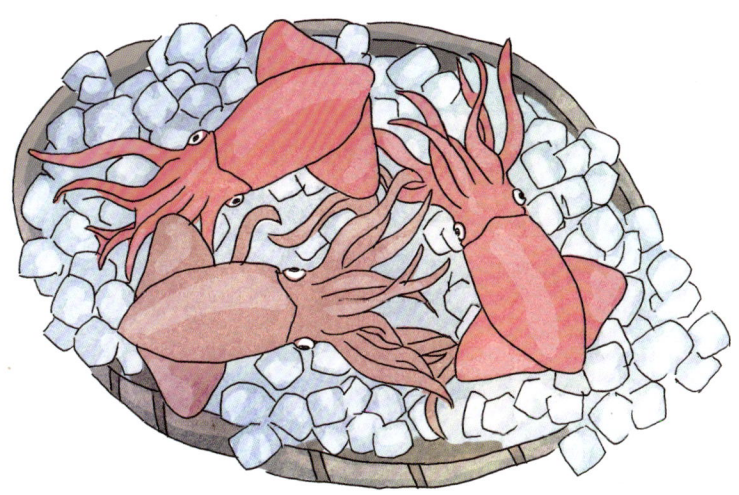

You will see crab and squid.

31

A Caribbean Market

A *market* is a place to buy and sell things. There are all kinds of markets. In this book, Lalin and her family go to a Caribbean market. The *Caribbean* is a sea filled with island countries like Haiti, where Lalin's family is from.

When people move from one country to another, they're called *immigrants*. Immigrants move to a new country for many reasons, like for a job, for school, or to be near family. There are many good parts of being an immigrant, but there are hard parts too. One hard part is finding ingredients from your home country. Without those ingredients, you can't cook your favorite foods.

At a certain markets, you *can* find those ingredients. And that's why markets can be important to immigrants. That's why the Caribbean market is important to Lalin's family.

At a Caribbean market, you can find ingredients like djon djon and jackfruit.

Ask your reader some questions like...

- What happened in this book?

- How did Lalin find help when she got lost?

- Turn to page 22. What do you think Lalin said to her mom and her sister when she found them?

- In this book, Lalin feels curious about all the things around her at the market. Where is a place that makes you feel curious like that?